D1109367

music to my eyes

music to my eyes

by Alfred Bendiner

UNIVERSITY OF PENNSYLVANIA PRESS

PHILADELPHIA · 1952

TO SERGEI RACHMANINOFF

All credit to Betty; to the late Paul Cranston; to Henry Pleasants; to the Philadelphia Evening Bulletin; the late lamented Philadelphia Record; the Washington Times-Herald; and the following ladies and gentlemen of the Arts who posed for these tributes to their abilities.

Sergei Rachmaninoff	Robert Casadesus	William Kincaid
Arturo Toscanini	Myra Hess	Marcel Tabuteau
Serge Koussevitsky	Guiomar Novaës	Kirsten Flagstad
Leopold Stokowski	William Kapell	Helen Traubel
Pierre Monteux	José Iturbi	Lily Pons
Dimitri Mitropoulos	Oscar Levant	Marian Anderson
Eugene Ormandy	Fritz Kreisler	Ezio Pinza
Bruno Walter	Jascha Heifetz	Dorothy Maynor
Charles Munch	Joseph Szigeti	Lauritz Melchior
Thomas Beecham	Nathan Milstein	Rose Bampton
Ernest Ansermet	Yehudi Menuhin	Jan Peerce
Leonard Bernstein	Mischa Elman	Licia Albanese
Sigmund Romberg	Erica Morini	Bidu Sayão
Vladimir Horowitz	Zino Francescatti	James Melton
Artur Rubinstein	Efrem Zimbalist	Fritz Reiner
Rudolf Serkin	Gregor Piatigorsky	Alicia Markova
Igor Stravinsky	William Primrose	Anton Dolin

music to my eyes

When I was a boy, my Uncle Arthur Hartmann was a famous violinist. He wore to his concerts a long velvet suit with half a dozen medals, and a yellow sash tied around his middle. He had his hair cut to look like the great Ysaye. After every concert he ate nothing but hot-house grapes—at least that was what I was told. We all worshipped and revered the great Uncle Arthur. Whenever he had a photograph taken, it was always in a soulful attitude with his index finger poking a hole in his cheek, and in his right hand a violin which my family insisted was one of the earliest and best Stradivariuses.

Before we were old enough to count our fingers we had to take lessons on the violin and become little Uncle Arthurs. I remember my teacher very well—a man who always smelled of pomade and beat my fingers and gave me sourballs to suck so I wouldn't cry too loud and make him lose his job.

My father stood the crying for two years, then sold the violins back to the pawnshops and decided that we were not going to be musicians. I suppose this is the childhood scar that I have inherited for psychiatrists to study in later life; it gave me a distinct dislike for music, and I kept away from it as long as possible.

During the Depression I turned to the newspaper business, doing caricatures for one of the papers. I had hoped to draw just theatre people, but soon I was catapulted into the dark mysteries of the world of music. My editor was a round rough-hewn fellow who played

the horses every day and didn't know or care about music or musicians; but since he had a music critic who covered the concerts and he was tired of photographs, I sold him the idea that I could do a caricature of the musician while he was playing, and have the drawing ready for him to publish along with the review the next day. This struck him as a grand idea. The main reason, I found out later, was that every day when a concert was played I got a pay check which he could use to bet on the horses. Somehow or other, though he never won, I was always repaid.

The problem was to fill a two-column space, and it was my job to go to the concert, watch the conductor or soloist until he got into a two-column attitude, come back to the office and make my drawing. This had to be ready in time for the engravers to make the cut and have it set in the paper to appear alongside the review of the concert. If I had been Picasso and hadn't hit that deadline or filled that two-column space exactly, my drawing would have been of no value to the newspaper.

Nothing in this book may be construed as expressing an opinion of the abilities of the ladies and gentlemen as musicians. There are plenty of know-it-alls who write books on that subject. I have caricatured them in word and line only because of their high position in the world of music. I hope they will take it in the spirit of good humor which is the sole intention of this book.

I dedicate this book to Rachmaninoff, who changed my early impression that a musician must look like Ysaye and wear velvet pants. Rachmaninoff wore a cropped haircut above a leather face and an iron suit. He could have been mistaken for a doctor, lawyer, or Indian chief. He was a very kind man, and when he sat for me he was quiet and ringed the floor around him with cigarette butts. As he walked on stage half bent over, with his arms dangling to his knees, he looked like a Brady photograph of Lincoln without the whiskers. Which again proves that appearances belie an innate sense of beauty.

To me Rachmaninoff was the greatest of them all. He not only was a composer, a pianist, and a conductor, but he also made a good caricature. After all, I was only there to judge his phiz, but unfortunately the editor thought differently. When he saw my caricature in the first edition he yanked it out because he thought nobody could look that ugly. Luckily for me, the art critics didn't agree with him, and prints of the lithograph — the last drawing made of him—are in several museums and collections.

Sergei Rachmaninoff

After Rachmaninoff, I'll take Toscanini. He is a great conductor, and he makes a good caricature. He is very near-sighted, and this affliction not only gives him a curious stance on the podium, but has forced him to memorize all scores. Conducting without a score has now been affected by a number of other conductors who can see perfectly well. Toscanini never uses one when conducting a concert, but I have seen him use a score in rehearsing the orchestra. He would suddenly stop in the middle of a composition and point to a violinist in the twenty-third bank of fiddles and tell him that he played a quarter note wrong. The violinist would stand with his score in hand; Toscanini would lift his score to his nose; and the two would compare quarter notes, make changes, and the rehearsal would go on.

Next to the conductor who always threw his watch at the orchestra during rehearsals and had it break all over the stage, I believe that Toscanini has the highest rating for breaking batons over his podium, score, and everywhere else, for no apparent reason. The time I saw him break one they weren't even playing an Italian composition.

Toscanini looks like a frail old man, but he must have great physical strength to beat out a full symphony.

Arturo Toscanini

Koussevitsky was the caricaturist's dream come true. He would get into such a stew over some minor composition that he would leave the podium completely worn out, perspiring heavily with his face the color of a boiled lobster. His attendant would wrap around him a big cloak, and the Maestro would stand in the wings adjusting a pair of spectacles that hadn't been worn since Benjamin Franklin put them in a museum case. He was a lovable old boy.

During the War when everything was rationed, including those specially padded coaches for musicians, the Boston Symphony had to ride in the ordinary coaches and stand in line for dinner. Koussevitsky adjusted his great cloak and stood in line behind a lot of other important people. A waiter saw him, beckoned to him, gave him a table, dusted it off, and went back to place his order. The head waiter called the waiter over and said, "What's the idea taking that white-haired man out of line before all those very important people ahead of him? Who do you think you are and who's he anyhow?" The waiter said, "Don't you know who that is? That's the great Serge Koussevitsky." "Who's he?" retorted the head waiter. "Why, he's the conductor of the Boston Symphony Orchestra. He's the white man's Duke Ellington."

Serge Koussevitsky

Then there is Stokowski. I had to make this drawing through a peep hole in the curtain because I wasn't allowed out front by orders of the great Maestro, but I've seen him conduct often enough to make a caricature of him. He is the Beau Brummell of conductors, impeccably tailored and coiffeured, and has done wonders with a big nose. Stokowski just couldn't keep his hands on the little white wand; he was one of the first to get rid of the baton and introduce ballet dancing into conducting. His instinct for showmanship was evidenced in the studied gestures of his hands which made you think they really were beautiful and that his fingers really were long and tapering. Now and then he would have to have the clavichord to monkey with while he was conducting the orchestra with the other hand. He was a great one for innovations. Theremin—remember? A man waving his hands in front of a vibrating stick that produced a musical-saw effect. The color organ with all kinds of flashes of colors and lights to prove that music was made for the gods. There were bird paintings on the backdrops, a sparkling aluminum podium and chairs, and costly experiments like "Oedipus" with Buffano's twenty-foot marionettes, crazy "Wozzek," and Chavez' turkey "H. P."

He loved to bawl out little old ladies for clapping or coughing, and if anyone dared to hiss the goofiest of novelty compositions all hell would break loose in cultivated Polish.

Leopold Stokowski

Pierre Monteux is another of my favorites to caricature. He still holds to a hair-do with a bird's nest in the back, and sports a long bushy gay-nineties moustache. He is one of the most charming and humorous of men, seemingly ageless and indefatigable. I remember seeing him beat out a concert in San Francisco where he and the audience were worn out, but when I went back to the hotel, there was Pierre Monteux walking his dog as any ordinary man would have to do before he went to bed. It was the funniest sight to see a little black man leading a little black dog all over the hills of San Francisco. He has not lost the spirit of his early days when he conducted the Diaghilev Ballet in Paris. He conducts an orchestra like a kid wheeling a hoop down the street. When the hoop veers, he brings it in line with a gentle motion of his stick.

Pierre Monteux

Dimitri Mitropoulos is hard to caricature. He looks and conducts like a long bird, and since I don't know anything about music, I've often wondered how the musicians can tell on which stroke of his shaky hands to blow that little note.

I wish he were not so interesting to watch, because I love listening to him.

I asked some of the boys how they managed with guest conductors, and one of them said, "It's like a bad headache or a week-end hangover. You know that by Tuesday everything will be back to normal."

Dimitri Mitropoulos

I publish this caricature of Eugene Ormandy because he likes it so well. It hangs in his dressing room, and he says it is not a caricature but a portrait showing how modest he is and how much credit he gives to his orchestra and his soloist. Ormandy took on the difficult job of following Stokowski at the Philadelphia Orchestra, not only as a musician but as a sartorially splendid figure. Whenever he goes on or off stage he feels his shirt cuffs to see if they are still there. Ormandy always looks much more scared of the crowd than they are of him; he's forever tugging at some bit of his sartorial splendor, and while his tailor has done a good job on the back of his coat, he can't quite hold his rear in yet. When Stokowski abandoned the stick so did he, and when Toscanini started memorizing scores so did Ormandy; but he is one of the most capable of conductors and is loved particularly by every soloist. They are loud in their praise of the way he lets them do their part; even when they overplay he keeps his orchestra in the background.

Eugene Ormandy

If you like German music your dish is Bruno Walter, who looks, acts, and plays exactly like everything you expect of the Germans. Early in life he acquired two black eyes which he has scrupulously maintained ever since. They stick out like two coals in his cropped white head.

The going is heavy, and if there is anything that puts me to sleep it's Wagner. The long dreary passages while waiting for Walter to fall into a two-column attitude would find me half asleep in one of the best seats in the house, with everybody shushing.

I know the public hates to have the impression of its heroes ruined, but these maestros off stage really behave like normal human beings. I remember another conductor who was so offended by my caricature of him that he wanted me immediately fired from the paper. The editor merely looked up from his desk and said, "Never draw the so-and-so again," and I didn't for several years. Finally the publicity department complained, and the editor said, "If you ever get a little hole in the top of one of the drawings put him in there." A few concerts later, we had a thin soloist who wouldn't get into a two-column attitude, so I drew the caricature of the soloist on one half of the space, and the conductor on the other. When that drawing appeared, the conductor sent me a glowing letter and asked if he could have the original drawing; however, if I sent him the original would I please cut the soloist off the other half?

Bruno Walter

One of the most difficult assignments ever handed to a conductor of an orchestra is the one Munch has undertaken with the Boston Symphony. He followed Koussevitsky, who besides being a great podium potentate and a great favorite with the ladies was a Russian, so that all Bostonians, beside speaking Bostonian, spoke Bostonian with a Russian accent. Now along comes a quiet, sedate conductor who does very little posing and is thoroughly competent. He doesn't show off and he speaks French; now everybody in Boston is having to learn French with a Boston accent, including Munch.

Speaking of accents, Hilsberg tried to learn American after the boys kidded him about trying to announce "Yonkey Duddel" on a children's program; but then he found out that to be a successful conductor you must also have a successful accent.

When the kids ran out on another conductor, he held up his hands and screamed, "Wait, leetle children, wait pliz. I am having big surprise in storage for you!"

Charles Munch

The debonaire Sir Thomas Beecham is always rewarding to fluttery American women. He is an impeccably dressed gentleman with waxed moustache and goatee, and looks for all the world like an early American magician. He has the charming habit of keeping seven or eight batons stuck in the edge of his cellist's desk so that when he breaks one he always has another handy.

Beecham is also a favorite with the musicians. When the Philadelphia Orchestra played in England, he visited one of the rehearsals and was greeted warmly by Ormandy and the orchestra. As he beamed on the boys, he noted that ladies were now members of the orchestra. He remarked on this change and asked Ormandy how everything was going. "Fine," said Ormandy. "No complications?" asked Beecham. "None whatever," replied Ormandy. "What a pity!" commented Beecham.

Thomas Beecham

Ansermet answered this caricaturist's dream when he fell off the podium. If you had dozed through as many concerts as I have, listening to Beethoven, Bach, Brahms, and all the other B's, you would realize that this was the moment you had waited for. You shouldn't fall off a podium when you look like Foxy Grandpa wearing a little white moustache and beard, and have a bald head that shines above the middle of the orchestra.

The concertmaster caught Ansermet on the end of his bow and pushed him back on the podium like the press boys pushing Dempsey back into the ring after Firpo had knocked him out of it. After he regained his composure he conducted as well as any other maestro. I understand that he has given his all for Stravinsky through Switzerland and France, and helped make him a world figure.

Ernest Ansermet

Leonard Bernstein

I suppose Bernstein is great, but he looks and acts like an old-fashioned conductor; his hair goes all over the place; he kicks the platform, beats time with his foot, and goes into the funniest stances for a fully designed and well-organized orchestra conductor. Of course I imagine a lot of this maneuvering is in imitation of his teacher, Papa Koussevitsky. I made this drawing of him from the directors' box surrounded by sixteen maestros all hoping he'd fall on his face.

If you had never seen Sigmund Romberg, but only heard his compositions, you were due for a great shock. Romberg wrote the most beautiful, lilting, popular waltzes, love songs, wonderful tuneful melodies; everything you expect of a composer for the people. But when he bounced on the stage, instead of a thin poetic-looking lover you had a gray, balding, middle-aged, fat, bouncing, jolly, unromantic little man. He took the two steps up to the podium in one jump and conducted like a graceful elephant poised on his toes, swinging his baton and dancing around as if he too were doing one of the waltzes for which he was so famous. If anything, he looked like a round butter ball. I thought it was great. I loved to see this change in pace from the dour conductor of the concert stage to the gay, popular music master. After all, music wasn't always so solemn. Even I can remember Willow Grove Park and some of the less austere music halls where there was enough light to see your beer.

Sigmund Romberg

All the joy in listening to music has been spoiled by having those dreary, dark concert halls with impossibly upholstered seats that you can't sit in for three hours. The audience comes in gay, laughing, having had a good meal and a couple of Martinis, and in festive mood is suddenly doused into impenetrable gloom. With a hundred musicians playing at full blast on the stage, no one is allowed to cough or even think aloud. The audience sits on the edge of its hard seats as if a miracle is being performed. The listeners are afraid to make any motion or sound of appreciation of what's going on and look exactly the same whether they are hearing the serious "Götterdämmerung" or the amusing "Till Eulenspiegel." The next time you go to a concert, look around. All those who are not asleep are looking intently forward into the blinding light which covers the face of an orchestra; I am sure that most of them are thinking about whether they left the front door unlocked or the gin bottle uncorked. I doubt if anybody in the audience can sit through a whole concert and listen to every note and enjoy it thoroughly. The people who enjoy a concert are the members of the orchestra themselves. If you are ever fortunate enough to go backstage when the orchestra comes off, you will find them all in good humor. Young and old, the best audience is at Children's Concerts. I have drawn at Children's Concerts as "soloist" with the orchestra. While they played the "Carnival of the Animals," I drew the animals. They played the "Nutcracker Suite" and I drew the little dancers from the local schools who came out and danced the numbers. As I gazed out across that sea of faces it looked like a microscope slide very highly populated with bacteria; everything was in motion; kids were running up and down the aisles to the washrooms; those who weren't throwing papers at each other were throwing them at the stage; they were all laughing at the right time and enjoying themselves. The orchestra kept on playing right through all this jumble of sounds. When they got through, I asked the conductor and the orchestra men how they liked it. They told me to a man that they loved playing Children's Concerts; they realized that the audience was right with them and having as much fun as they were.

On Friday afternoons the concert is given before a group of survivors who have inherited their seats from the family, and there is never a seat for sale. There are very few men in the audience, and the affair is a social event as much as a display of musicianship. On Saturday nights the big business men are dragged there by their wives, and spend most of the time waiting for the intermission so they can talk business to each other in the foyer. Afterwards they spend half of Saturday night at a dull musicians' party. On Monday night the musicians and the students and the school teachers all gather and hang on every note.

In addition to regular soloists, the orchestra must have innovations. For one of these you suffer through a very slight bit called "Peter and the Wolf." Every grandfather who has read a child a story must realize what a complete bore he is, but that doesn't seem to stop the voices from reciting this to the accompaniment of the best orchestras in the country.

Since this book is dedicated to Rachmaninoff, it's high time we got to the pianists.

For the caricaturist, as well as the audience, the appearance of a piano soloist with orchestra is a great event. Usually he comes right after the intermission or follows the opening number of a concert, and gives everybody a breather. There is always a lot of commotion on the stage. Everybody is incommoded—the violinists move back, the stage doors flop open, and at least four husky union hands in various stages of undress wheel out the big black monster and raise its ungainly flap which completely blots out half of the orchestra and the antics of the conductor. Then one official stage hand carries in the seat of office, which is an ugly padded bench. No concert pianist would think of using an ordinary stool. While this performance is going on, the audience has a wonderful time gossiping and jabbering at a great rate, or completely engrossed in the mechanics on the stage. I have even heard them applaud the piano movers as they walked solemnly to the wings. Then the maestro mounts the podium. The pianist, dressed in the same

dreary evening clothes, comes on stage, nervously screws himself up and down on his piano bench and wipes his hands a couple of hundred times, and finally signals to the conductor that he is ready.

When the pianist is soloist without an orchestra, all the mechanics of moving are completed before the audience arrives, and the soloist reduces the monster to his will alone on a mighty stage with a backdrop which is usually a leftover curtain from some forgotten opera. The one I'm most accustomed to shows the interior of a drawing room with doors about eight miles high looking out upon a frowsy English garden. Flanking these enormous entry doors are two little tables with painted bowls of flowers. If you get tired of listening to the pianist, you can figure out what new cracks have developed in the curtain in the last thirty years. Once in a while, to relieve the monotony of the soloist, there is a page turner who sits black, ominous, and rigid, waiting for the exact moment when he should *turn*.

I liked the assignment of doing Vladimir Horowitz, another good caricature of a face. I enjoyed his dressing room, which was always a perfect bedlam. It looked like the Russian pictures of the village scene, with a samovar going full tilt and the floor all strewn with chewed sunflower seeds. The whole family was there gabbling away, while Horowitz warmed his hands before going out to hit the cold keys of the piano.

Horowitz looks as if the "Danse Macabre" was written just for him—a pale nervous bone-bag of a man, all full of wire and jitters. He doesn't suffer nearly as much as he appears to.

Vladimir Horowitz

Artur Rubinstein is a fatty with a large head of hair that looks like curled pipe cleaners. Somebody must have told him that he looked and played like Brahms, and he has taken it so to heart that he has had himself photographed to look like the famous painting of Brahms at the piano, cigar and all. I don't know that he is the greatest living pianist, but he certainly is a set-up for the caricaturist.

Artur Rubinstein

One of the corniest publicity stunts ever perpetrated on a musician was when they gave Serkin a tractor on the stage of the Academy of Music. Of all the goofy ideas, this seems like the number one piece of idiocy, but I suppose it made a good picture in the papers.

Of all the unseated pianists, Serkin is the most nervous of them all; when he comes on stage he fiddles for about five minutes whirling himself up and down on the piano stool and warming his hands on the keys. Then, with a jerk of his head, he's off. Between bouncing up and down and banging on the keys with his full strength, he and the audience seem worn out by the time he is through with one little number.

Serkin should ride a piano seat like a Toulouse-Lautrec jockey, with just enough light between the two seats to make an artistic production.

Rudolf Serkin

I made this drawing of Stravinsky the Great when he appeared in Philadelphia prior to the publication of his book, and sent him the caricature and asked him to approve it. He sent back the caricature unopened, with a wonderful letter that said he never looked at caricatures, never looked at pictures of himself, wouldn't sign or approve anything.

A couple of years ago, the French Government acquired some of my prints for the permanent collection in the Cabinet des Estampes. Among them were lithographs of musicians, and now they repose in the bottom vaults of the Bibliothèque Nationale waiting for me to die. When I came back to the States I met one of these musicians—not Stravinsky—and was very happy to tell him all this. I said, "Now you see, in spite of the fact that you didn't like that caricature I made of you, you're in the Louvre." He replied, "Why not? I should have been in there long ago."

Igor
Stravinsky

Casadesus, or Casa-de-sus, or however you're supposed to pronounce it, is much too large a man to play an ordinary piano. He makes it look childish, the way Jackie Robinson makes baseball look childish. I have seen him come on stage several times, and thought he was about to sell United States Government bonds or the Community Chest. Of course, when he sits down at the piano, he is a beautiful player and a wonderful musician, and I hope some day they'll build a piano to his size so that he looks in key with it.

Robert
Casadesus

Myra Hess is lavender and old lace, and one of the old school of piano playing which was made famous in the caricatures of the nineties, where everybody held their arms very stiff, their wrists broken at a right angle, their fingers very straight, and hit the keys in the most difficult tortured attitudes. She is one of the few lady pianists, but if you close your eyes, she sounds like a man.

Myra Hess

At the other end of the scale, Guiomar Novaës, a much younger pianist, is a Brazilian belle who carries her weight beautifully to the piano, sits down and plays with enormous charm. She shows great sympathy for the works of Octavio Pinto, her late husband.

Guiomar Novaës

William Kapell is another jumpy pianist who won't relax and let it come to you. He wears a Bushman hair coif and looks pale and embarrassingly nervous. He's forever mopping his forehead or his hands with his handkerchief, and you think he's never going to get it back into his pocket in time to come in on his next part. He dashes on stage, plays like a marionette pianist—jerks his mane up and down as if his head was on a wire—and dashes off.

William Kapell

Bendiner

José Iturbi

José Iturbi, in order to change the pace a bit, tries the old stunt of playing the piano and conducting the orchestra at the same time. It is the most complicated mess I have ever seen, and one of the most distracting.

As if there weren't enough good pianists on the stage without any doubling-in-brass efforts, every once in a while we get treated to a spot man who does well on the piano and something else either on the microphone or with his hands. Oscar Levant, for instance, having written a know-it-all book about music and musicians and appeared on radio and in the movies, is now an authority on Gershwin, particularly the "Rhapsody in Blue." I like the "Rhapsody in Blue"; I heard Gershwin play it when he was touring with Paul Whiteman about twenty-five years ago. There was a repertoire of the beginnings of jazz with the Dixieland Jazz Band. Finally Gershwin appeared and played his complete "Rhapsody in Blue," which you seldom hear.

Levant has taken over the Gershwin tradition, playing that one number. He does it beautifully, but beside that you get a lot of hand-waving, shaking and talking to the microphone; everything except straight piano playing of another number.

Oscar Levant

If there is anything dreary in this world, it's a violin soloist all alone on a great big stage. One should never go to a violin concert unless he's lost his dog, or his wife is lying in bed with a sacroiliac, or if there is any real reason to have a good cry. There is nothing so monotonous as a violin soloist scratching away and upsetting everybody's normal routine of life, making them all sad and serious when they really ought to be gay.

The violin pictures that I remember with dancers in the village are all gone, and this is the modern picture of the little fiddler: the lights go down and out comes a somber figure in black; he tucks his little fiddle under his chin, signals the accompanist, and saws away for dear life until ten-thirty arrives. Everybody is worn out, their handkerchiefs are all full, and they are ready to go home and continue crying for the rest of the night.

I like to remember Kreisler as a sort of one-man United Nations. When I was young, he returned to this country an alien enemy after the First World War, when everybody was hating Germans and Austrians, but he worked himself into the hearts of all the people. Beside being a fine player he was always very courteous, polite, and good-humored.

Fritz Kreisler

Heifetz always received the press with a dead pan, particularly me. He was cold and I always hated to make a drawing of him. I tried to be nice to him, but he never changed his expression.

There used to be a prize-fighter named Benny Leonard who was cold, calculating, and hard-working. He walked into the ring, proceeded to go through as many rounds as was necessary to knock out his opponent, and left the ring without having his hair mussed. I always appreciated his great style, accuracy, and precision. I once told Heifetz that he reminded me very much of Benny Leonard. It was supposed to be a compliment. Heifetz held up his hands and said to me, "Do these look to you like prize-fighter's hands?" I must hand it to him for one thing, though. He is trying to change that dreary old repertoire of the violin concert and put some new pieces before the public.

Jascha Heifetz

Joseph Szigeti is the fiddler's fiddler, and they tell me he is the most accomplished violinist of them all, but he made life difficult waiting for him to fill two columns. He is built like a broomstick and stands as if he practiced in a telephone booth. This German school of bowing with the elbow pinned against the ribs and the wrist doing all the work is a great relief from the Leopold Auer students of Russian gymnastics. Rigid bowing is acquired by holding a book under your bowing arm or pinning your elbow to your pants while you play.

There was a conductor who claimed he had such a sensitive ear that he had to tune all the violins in the orchestra himself. The boys foxed him. They let him tune one fiddle and then passed the same fiddle to each man as he went in, so the conductor innocently tuned the same violin about forty times.

Joseph Szigeti

Whenever Milstein was scheduled to play, I had an easy time of it. He's one of the hair-in-the-eye boys; he wears a long forelock that bounces right across his face and cuts out all his features. I never can understand why violinists always save that forelock, unless they hope in their old age to make a bow of it. I never think of Milstein without Piatigorsky alongside of him. I have seen them several times playing a duet together. It's a wonderful sight—the great big Piatigorsky wrapped around his cello pushing his great big spidery elbows into poor little Milstein's side as he scratches away on his violin. I saw Milstein once long after I had made a drawing of the two of them, and he said, "I hope some day you'll make a drawing of me poking Piatigorsky in the ribs instead of always having Piat pushing me off the stage."

Nathan Milstein

Yehudi Menuhin has grown to full and complete stature in music with the same effectiveness that he had as a child prodigy. I remembered him, of course, as most of us do, from the time his father carried him on with his little fiddle, to now when he still looks fat and pinkish. The first time I was assigned to make a drawing of Menuhin, he appeared in a white suit and was bathed in a golden light, so when I drew him I put a little pair of wings on him to make him look like an angel. The editors said that was sacrilegious, and immediately ripped it out of the paper.

Yehudi Menuhin

And then there is Mischa Elman, who, after every little number hangs his head on the side like a little boy who has done something wrong waiting for the audience to stop clapping as if it was really nothing.

Beside being a great violinist, he is a non-stop talker. I can't understand why these Russian players can't have real names like everybody else. You have to remember who Jascha, Sascha, Mischa, Tascha, and Grisha all are in order to be on drawing acquaintance with them.

Mischa Elman

Erica Morini was declared the "peer of the greatest of her male colleagues" a few years ago. She looks like a violinist — deep, sad and somber — and, of course, dresses in solid black like a Piero di Cosimo figure.

Erica Morini

Zino Francescatti, one of the outstanding violinists, is a simple, unaffected musician to interview and to draw. He plays beautifully in a businesslike way without any great effects or flourishes, and maybe that's what's the matter with him. He is a great favorite of violinists, however, while the general public doesn't support him too well.

Zino Francescatti

Efrem Zimbalist is not only a good solid player but a relief from the waving violinists. He stands like a businessman and goes through the compositions without very much emotion, figuratively speaking. He has also been a great teacher, and now and then he gets up on the podium, unable to resist being a conductor.

For no good reason, he reminds me of the story of the violinist who was playing in London as a soloist. When he had completed his solo, a friend of his went back stage to greet him. The orchestra had struck up "God Save the King" as their normal finale, and there was the violinist standing at rigid attention with his violin at his side, when my friend walked in. The violinist looked at him and said, "Isn't it wonderful! They are playing 'My Country 'Tis of Thee' in my honor."

Efrem Zimbalist

BENDINER

Piatigorsky is the tallest cellist of them all. He makes the cello look like a watch-charm fiddle, and with true modesty he carries it in, in his left hand, high over the heads of the orchestra. I thought this was an affectation and I drew him that way, but when I showed him the drawing he said that he didn't realize he was doing that at all.

If you think you suffer listening to a whole evening of violin solo playing, you ought to be forced to sit through a whole evening of cello. By that time you're so far down in the depths that the state of the world seems rosy in comparison. I had a hard time getting this assignment because the editor didn't think cellos looked good in the paper!

Piatigorsky has told this story on himself often, but I still think it's a good one. He was playing a concert one night when right in the middle of fingering his fine passages he heard a lot of roaring of animals somewhere around. He kept on playing, looking furtively around to see if a lion had escaped into the audience, and as soon as the number was finished he raced backstage to find out what the trouble was. The stage manager said that he *had* heard lions, that after his concert they were striking the set and setting up for a circus that had come into the auditorium and was playing there the next night, and they had the lions stored in cages down in the basement.

Piatigorsky went back and played his next number, and said to the audience, "They *are* lions that you hear, but can I help it if the animals appreciate my great music?"

Gregor Piatigorsky

Since I have been so generous in giving you pictures of the violin soloists, and making long groans about the dark halls of the violin concerts, and giving you a picture of the cello soloist, you might as well have the middle man, the viola player. The viola is bigger than a violin and smaller than a cello, so it's stuck up under the chin, and you would expect that the man who had the divine right to play this instrument would look large enough for it.

Here is the greatest violist of them all, a fairly short man with a busted nose and a Scott Fitzgerald school haircut, who plays like a god—Mr. William Primrose. His other distinction is that he is one of the few Englishmen who have attained the rank of soloist on the American platform.

William Primrose

I cannot show caricatures of all the many fine first desk players who are the backbone of the orchestra, so I have picked two to represent them all. Billy Kincaid is the world's best flute player and the first desk in the Philadelphia Orchestra. Besides that, he looks like a flute player. He should have posed for the flute player in the "Spirit of '76." Kincaid looks like a fat faun when he isn't trying to look like George Washington; he has a great big mane of white hair which is combed straight in the air, and after blowing a whole evening on that platinum flute he has the most florid red face you have ever seen.

Kincaid and Tabuteau have backed up the strings of the Philadelphia Orchestra for years, and every once in a while come up front as soloists.

William Kincaid

Marcel Tabuteau

Tabuteau looks and behaves exactly the way every Frenchman is supposed to look and behave for public appreciation. While everybody else gets bald or gray after enough years, Tabuteau maintains a black coif and big lushy black eyebrows, all of which look well with that black oboe he blows on.

The true test of trying the audience's patience is to have three maestros playing at the same time, without cutting each others' throats. This was done successfully a couple of years ago when the Brahms trio was played by Heifetz, Rubinstein, and Piatigorsky. The production was a smooth, beautiful rendition, but from the caricaturist's point of view they behaved like the three Marx Brothers.

A soloist told me a story about his nephew, whose mother wrote him that her son had got 100 in a music test and would be a great musician like his uncle, so please send him a trumpet because his father was a member of the American Legion and loved to hear Taps.

The trumpet player told him that anybody with two heads could play a trumpet, and a kid who got 100 in a music test knew too much about music to be a trumpet player.

The next time the soloist was in town he went to see his sister and started playing the test questions for the boy. When he played "The Flight of the Bumblebee" the kid called it "The Dance of the Sugar Plum Fairies." When he played "The Dance of the Sugar Plum Fairies" the boy called it "The Sorcerer's Apprentice," and so on. The soloist put down his instrument and said, "You got them all wrong. How did you ever get 100 in this test?" "Well," the kid said, "we recognize them different. 'The Flight of the Bumblebee' record has got a crack in it. 'The Dance of the Sugar Plum Fairies' has a high screech." So the soloist knew he was dumb enough to be a trumpet player and sent him a trumpet for a Bar-mitzvah present.

And now he has a pupil.

Jascha Heifetz, Artur Rubinstein & Gregor Piatigorsky

The voice accompanied by the orchestra, or solo, is a great favorite of the culture vultures. It brings out the mother instinct, I suppose—since everybody has been put to sleep by his mama's tired voice.

The stage voice is far from soporific—it's an agony job. I suppose it is difficult to sing, breathe, and carry a lot of weight and be effective without contortions. Besides, it must rack the couturiers to design those dresses. The gentlemen have it easy, since a simple black-crow suit falls back into place after the shadow boxing, but the poor soprano has to go through an evening of heavy breathing, arm-waving and posturing, and finally come to quiet rest with every zipper holding and no wrinkles. No lady soloist would dare sing in a simple gown. You are usually treated to a large woman decked out in a creation which makes her look even larger, which must glitter and swish and be too colorful.

Kirsten Flagstad is a great figure of a voice. She certainly is the All-Wagnerian fullback of our time. If there hadn't been a war she probably would have been pulled through the streets in an open carriage by her admirers and had roses thrown at her, but unfortunately things didn't work out that way for her.

Kirsten Flagstad

There seems to be a lot of discussion about who is a bigger singer, Flagstad or Traubel, but in the over-all portrait Traubel looks bigger.

As if she weren't large enough already, she once appeared in a solid gold sparkling gown that gave everybody the shivers, not only listening to her but watching her, and alongside the orchestra she looked like a towering figure of the heavyweight Venus.

When she appears as soloist with the Philadelphia Orchestra, Ormandy shrinks and goes into his shy act, waiting with a forced patience until her ladyship closes her little book and departs.

Ed Schloss, the critic, once said to Ormandy, "Gene, you know you ought not to be so shy about these things, and I'll tell you how to solve the whole problem and everybody will love it. The next time Helen Traubel comes to sing here let her carry you on, in the crook of her arm."

Helen Traubel & Eugene Ormandy

Lily Pons did a lot for opera. She is a demure, good-looking charmer, and a great relief from the Wagnerian war-horses. When she sang in "Daughter of the Regiment" with big Baccaloni, she really looked like something a soldier might adopt.

During the war she and her husband André Kostelanetz toured the outlying areas. In India they scared the daylights out of her by that old gag of taking her temperature without shaking the thermometer down. When she took it out of her mouth, it registered 108; the scream which followed was in perfect key but too high, even for her.

She's still cute.

Lily Pons

Marian Anderson is a very difficult subject to caricature. She grimaces, she over-accentuates with facial contortions, she closes her eyes and is always very serious and almost in a crying mood.

Marian Anderson

Ezio Pinza, besides being a great singer, is a handsome gent in an Italian way. By singing in "South Pacific" he raised the stock of the middle-aged lover, and all the pipe-smoking, carpet-slipper boys are buying Kinsey reports.

He profiles too much.

His English pronunciation sounds like the man who went to the Berlitz School to learn Italian, so he could speak English like Ezio Pinza.

Ezio Pinza

Dorothy Maynor is a particular favorite of mine, but she had one unerring failing when she was young: she insisted upon designing all the gowns she wore on the stage. They were awful. She had a little round figure to start with, and she affected plumes and billowy dresses that only made her look funny. But when the lights went down and she sang the beautiful "Depuis le Jour" from the opera "Louise," which had never been sung any better even by Mary Garden, I listened instead of looked, which I seldom did with other musicians. At the close of this moving performance the audience would tear the house down with applause, and Dorothy Maynor with complete naïveté and modesty would bow a couple of hundred times and salute the audience like a winning prize fighter.

It was cute, but the know-it-all boys in the back room soon worked her out of all that naturalness.

Dorothy Maynor

I am told that a famous Belgian doctor once made the apt remark, "The mind can only absorb as much as the seat can endure." He probably was one who was dragged by his wife to the opera and learned the hard way.

Opera is the great art form, and it also gives every college kid a chance to be a "super," so that later in life he can tell you that he "carried water" for the sopranos or carried a spear in "Aïda." He remembers Caruso and how much better he had sung than the present-day singers. I don't believe it. I can't remember who sang from one year to the next and certainly not how much worse than Caruso.

My friend Mahlon Yardley, who has been active in the audience for the past sixty years, tells me that I don't understand the idiom. If I don't understand it I can't understand how anybody else does. After all, you have four idioms to worry about when you go to an opera. You expect the finest presentation, the finest singing, the finest acting, and the finest stage direction and setting. Any one of these requires the most minute attention to detail all evening, so the net result for me is that I am completely confused. What I had to do was to find the finest two-column attitude that would express the whole sentiment of the opera so that the reader the next day could see that I had caught the most important moment of the most important of all operas. I used to bone up by reading a digest of the opera at dinner so that I could be in my seat early, all set to enjoy a whole evening of the finest

of everything, and try to remember the details of the most complicated Gilbert and Sullivanesque plot.

Usually the audience is much funnier than the opera itself. Almost everybody is late; they stumble down dark aisles, clamber down impossible steps, and there is a constant jumping up and down in the whole audience as if there was a permanent hot seat during the first act. The audience follows the opera with librettos and little pocket flashlights, and the opera house in the middle of a performance looks like a hive of glowworms trying to read what is happening on the stage.

They can hardly wait for it to end. When the lights go on, everybody adjusts opera glasses, stands up, looks around to see who's there, comments on what they're wearing, and watches for the newspaper photographers, to be sure to get in the social page. The major problem of this idiom is the one of languages. Americans who demand everything else to be translated into American, because they never know any other language, treat opera as something that is untranslatable. The operas that have been performed in English have been, for the most part, flops. It just seems that opera isn't opera unless it's in Italian, German, French, or Russian. They sit completely satisfied though not understanding one word of the most beautiful sentiments that are being expressed on the stage.

The opera "Aïda" has been packing them in since 1871, and gives everybody a break. It has brassy music and sweet stringy love passages, costumes, big scenery, ballet, and spectacles, and sometimes even elephants on stage embarrassing everybody. For eighty years "Aïda" has stood all kinds of tests and is still a good opener for a season.

Here is the final blast of Act II (take it slowly)—Rhadames the soldier (center) who has just returned from the wars, still loves Celeste Aïda, the slave girl (left of center), but the King (right of Rhadames) plays mean because he wants Rhadames for his daughter Amneris (right end). However, the horned gent on the left is Aïda's papa, Amonasro, who has just been brought home as a prisoner and doesn't want his daughter to show any sign of recognition.

At this point I always had to leave to make a drawing to hit that deadline, and I have never known how they untangle it all.

I think Wagner can best be exemplified by the adjective "Kolossal." It's wonderful if you like big cubes of women acting coy or meaty choruses shaking the paint off the ornamental plaster angels on the ceiling. The caricatures come out best if you just do a straight German portrait.

I have always felt that Wagner must have been a sadist at heart, because anyone who acts in his works has to go through some of the darnedest tortures so the show can go on.

I could go through all the "Ring" and back—but what's the use? Here is Miss Rhinemaiden of 1952-53 and forever. Her life on stage is a lot of hard work; besides being able to sing well, she has to stand on perilous paper rocks at shaky heights or help drag big armored heroes to heaven.

By about 9:30 I begin to feel my seat, and my wife is scrunching around in the darkness trying to find her shoes.

This is the big moment, and the last, in "Lohengrin." Mysterious Lo has appeared a couple of acts ago to disrupt everybody's knightly life and is now leaving in his boat pulled by his trusty swan (who turns out to be good-gracious Godfrey, a fair-haired boy) after the white dove of the Holy Grail flutters around Lo's head.

Well anyhow it's a great scene and a great problem for the artist. Here is Lauritz Melchior, the baby elephant of Wagner, playing Knight L. singing away at the top of his lungs while trying to balance himself on a kiddie car which is slowly yanked across the stage by a stuffed swan emitting clouds of stage dust. There flutters over Lo's head a white dove on a wire, and if everything holds, the curtain will be down quickly.

On the right Miss Rose Bampton mourns the passing hero.

Lauritz Melchior is the Mr. Big of the voice.

He can stand up to any Wagnerian soprano and blast back at her. Now that he has succumbed to the movie lure, he has to sing a lot of stuff beneath the great dignity of his proportions. As one critic suggested, it's like trying to kick a field goal with a tennis ball.

Lauritz Melchior & Rose Bampton

Now "Le Coq d'Or" is a very picturesque fairy tale and well worth the trouble. It's played as a ballet pantomime, with the text sung by the artists and a chorus.

It's all about a king who is given a golden cockerel to warn him of danger, and the bird pecks his skull out when he refuses to give the astrologer a cutie he has picked up on the battlefield . . . or something as simple and normal as that.

There are imaginative sets and costumes, and the singing is done in caricature. It is sung in Russian, and a six-year-old can understand what goes on without too much effort.

Jan Peerce as Marcel and Licia Albanese as Mimi in "La Boheme" are two underfed artistes of good old Paris who never have a cent and are always boiling soup in an attic room where there is about as much privacy as an army barracks.

This is the touching scene at the city gates of Paris early in the morning; it is snowing and cold to make life more complicated.

Of course, as soon as Marcel and Mimi see each other they bust out in a lovely duet without even a cup of coffee to help them get a start. All this charm wakes up all Paris, which has been dying to get those last forty winks.

Poor consumptive Mimi usually weighs in at 210, and soup-ridden Marcel at about 240.

Jan Peerce
Licia Albanese

"Butterfly" is a real tear-jerker, and they ran it on even during the recent unpleasantness because Miss Bidu Sayão San was here to sing it.

It plays hob with all those big Italian singers who crawl around on their knees to try to look like little geisha girls, crossing bridges and singing those piping tunes, and a great big American sailor boy, James Melton, loving a midget who is always singing at his groin.

The big nervous moment is when they set out a one-year-old baby waving an American flag and hope it holds until the curtain drops.

Bidu Sayão & James Melton

The hardest work at the opera on this side of the footlights is not done by the audience but by the orchestra, and particularly its conductor. The maestro of all of them in this respect is Fritz Reiner. You hardly ever see him except at the beginning of the third or fourth act when everybody is tired and wants to go home. Then he takes his little bow before the last act of the opera, turns, the house darkens, and you never see him again. However, he is in sole and complete control of everything that is going on; the music, the stage direction, and even that little guy in the box behind the black hood, over the footlights.

Fritz Reiner

I show this as my last drawing. It is a caricature of the famous ballet dancers Alicia Markova and Anton Dolin, intruded upon by the column supporting the balcony. I suppose that in my position I should have been a little more capable of taking the joke when it was on me. Unfortunately I had been buffeted around in all the uncomfortable seats for so long that the last straw was being seated behind the column. I told the editor that I could only draw what I saw, and he ran it. We received a lot of letters from indignant people asking how I had got their seat.

This caricature was the curtain to my career on one newspaper, and I close quietly with it.

Somebody once asked me to what I attribute my ability as a caricaturist, and I can only quote that immortal saying of the late lamented prize fighter Sam Langford: "I guess it's 'cause everything I eat is fried."

Alicia Markova & Anton Dolin